THE AUTHOR'S GUIDE TO MEDIA INTERVIEWS

ROB EAGAR

The Author's Guide to
Media Interviews

Published by Wildfire Marketing

Requests to publish excerpts from this book should be sent to:
Rob@Startawildfire.com

Cover design: Ron Dylnicki

❀ Created with Vellum

ENDORSEMENTS

"I recommend Rob Eagar to any author looking to take their book campaign to a higher level."

Dr. Gary Chapman - #1 *New York Times* bestselling author of *The Five Love Languages*

"Rob Eagar gets great results and strategically places authors in the right spaces. I'm happy with what Rob did for me, and I highly recommend him."

Dr. John Townsend - *New York Times* bestselling author of *Boundaries*

"Rob Eagar provided book marketing insights that I hadn't heard before. It was wonderful to speak with such a seasoned marketing pro."

Nir Eyal - *Wall Street Journal* bestselling author of *Hooked* and *Indistractable*

"Rob revolutionized how I market my novels and connect with readers. His Book Marketing Master Class gave me more fantastic ideas that I knew what to do with."

Dani Pettrey - Bestselling novelist with over 300,000 copies sold

"Rob Eagar's expertise helped me develop a new brand and create an exciting new website. It was beyond my expectations and included everything I asked for and more."

Wanda Brunstetter - 6-time *New York Times* bestselling novelist with over 12 million copies sold

"Rob Eagar knows how to use words and has very fine penmanship. You should really listen to him."

His Mother - English major who taught Rob to speak and write clearly

MY FREE GIFT FOR YOU

Get three e-books to help jumpstart your book sales for FREE:

Find Readers and Sell Books on a Shoestring Budget

Mastering Book Hooks for Authors

The Ultimate Book Marketing Plan Template for Authors

Join my email newsletter and get these three e-books. Each resource can be downloaded as a file to your computer or added to any e-reader device. You will also receive my weekly e-newsletter packed with free expert marketing advice for authors.

Download these three e-books for free today at:

https://www.startawildfire.com/free-ebooks-ag

INTRODUCTION: HOW I BLEW THE BIGGEST INTERVIEW OF MY LIFE

I published my first book in 2002, long before the rise of social media, the creation of podcasts, and the dominance of Amazon. A few months after my book's release, an opportunity came across my path that most authors would kill to receive.

Sitting in my office one day, the phone rang. When I answered, I was stunned to hear the caller say, "Hi, I'm a producer for the *CBS Early Show*. We'd like to interview you on our national TV program. Would you be interested?"

I was so shocked that I fumbled the phone and almost dropped it on the floor. I couldn't believe my ears.

"How did you find me?" I asked.

The producer responded, "We were doing research online and ran across your website. Could we send a camera crew to your location within the next six days?"

I was dumbfounded. The only professional thing I could think to say was "sure."

The producer replied, "Great, I'll send you an email with a few more details." Then, the call was over.

Six days later, a van loaded with camera equipment and a bunch of technical people showed up and knocked on my door. The technical director asked, "It's a beautiful day outside, so we've decided to interview you under a tree in your backyard. Is that okay?"

"Sure...no problem," I replied, as if I had any say in the matter.

Within 45 minutes, the camera gear was setup, microphones were tested, and a famous network correspondent drove up in a rental car who popped out ready to interview me.

I tried to remain calm, but the whole experience felt surreal. My wife stood nearby watching the scene. Neighbors were peering into my yard. Everyone was staring at me.

The correspondent asked a few prepared questions, and I tried to reply without sounding like a fool. Everything seemed to go by in a blur.

The camera crew recorded the conversation, which lasted no more than 10 minutes. Next, they quickly packed up their equipment, and the producer departed by saying my interview would air on CBS within a couple of weeks.

Ten days later, I turned on the television and saw my face being broadcast coast-to-coast across America. I was so excited by the exposure that I felt like I had just won the lottery!

My mom was proud. My friends thought I was famous. It seemed like one of those life-changing moments. I braced myself for an avalanche of notoriety and book sales. All of my author dreams were about to come true. Once my interview aired on national television, I waited for the success to wash over me.

And, then...nothing happened.

My phone didn't ring with any requests from people to buy my book. My email inbox didn't receive any new messages.

I went to bed and woke up the next day...but nothing happened.

I peeked at my book's Amazon sales ranking. Yet, it had barely changed from what it was before my interview aired.

The next day, again, nothing happened. No phone calls, no emails from adoring readers, and no change in my book sales.

This same pattern continued for over a week. More anticipation...more disappointment.

It took almost a month to finally accept reality. I had landed an interview on one of the biggest television shows in America and completely blown it.

At first, I blamed the program producers. My lack of book sales was their fault, because they didn't ask me better questions. Or, they didn't show my book cover on the TV screen. Or, they didn't mention my website address...on and on.

But, as I pondered what really happened, I couldn't deny that the true source of the problem was me. The disaster was my fault. I blew a golden opportunity, because I went into the media interview without a plan.

Worse, my ego was too inflated to think that I actually needed a strategy in order to maximize an interview. I assumed that my zeal would be infectious and the national TV exposure would rocket me onto the bestseller lists.

Boy, did I get a wakeup call. I swore to never make that same mistake again. Sometimes, pain is the best teacher.

Fortunately, I learned from my blunder, took charge of my marketing responsibilities, and eventually turned my author business into a thriving six-figure income.

My book wound up selling thousands of copies and remained on the shelf in Barnes & Noble bookstores for 10 years.

Long story short, I became such a successful author that other writers started asking me for marketing advice. Today, I work as a consultant who has taught over 1,000 authors how to increase their book sales.

Yet, as I coach authors, I meet too many who waste the same media opportunities that I did 20 years ago.

Have you ever squandered a lucky break with the media? Have you appeared on a TV program, radio show, or popular podcast but left with nothing to show for it?

No book sales...no follow-up interest...no self-confidence. It hurts, right?

Worse, are you so easily thrilled with just getting an interview that you forget to be purposeful with the opportunity? Instead, do you show up and try to "wing it" with spontaneity, because you hate to practice or plan ahead?

Allow me to shoot down a major media misconception right from the start:

Unless you're a mainstream celebrity, "winging it" during an interview will NEVER help you sell more books.

Sure, it's fun to tell your friends that you'll be on a popular TV program, podcast, or radio show. But, don't let your ego get in the way of doing the work to build your author platform. It takes forethought and preparation to get results out of a media appearance.

In this resource, I'm going to explain how to use media interviews to sell more books.

To be clear, this resource is NOT about how to get media interviews. Any author can secure interviews. All you have to do is reach out to enough podcast hosts or pay an expensive publicity firm. For example, if you want to appear on a podcast, follow these simple steps:

Step 1 – Use Google, iTunes, or the Apple Podcast app to research and identify podcasts that like to interview authors in your genre. (Pro tip: To save time, conduct your search by using the names of 2 – 3 bestselling authors in your genre.)

Step 2 – Once you identify podcasts that are right for you, go to the podcast's official website.

Step 3 – Most podcast websites have a "Contact Us" form or an email address displayed to send a message offering yourself as an interview guest. Use that contact information to inquire about an appearance and follow-up on your own.

Lining up podcast interviews is that simple. It's easy and free.

In contrast, if you want to appear on a radio or television show, the steps are even simpler. But, it will cost you a lot of money, usually at least $10,000. That's because you'll need to hire a publicity firm to pursue those types of interview requests on your behalf.

If you're unfamiliar with how the media industry works, you can't just call up *The NBC Today Show* or *NPR Radio* and ask for an appearance. Instead, you have to personally know the decision-makers at those programs and go through their trusted lines of communication. The best way to do that is by hiring a publicist who already knows the decision-makers and agrees to pitch you as an effective guest.

If you can afford the expensive fee of a PR agency, then do a Google search for "Book PR Agencies" or "Book Publicist." You'll find a listing of publicists who specialize in working with authors and new book campaigns.

Talk with at least 3 – 4 publicists before you make a final decision. Never hire a publicist without asking for samples of their past work or getting references from past clients. Otherwise, you could waste a ton of money.

Above all, don't expect a PR firm to give you any media training. Most publicists have never actually written a book or conducted an interview on their own. They're just middlemen who make connections for you with media producers and podcast hosts. They'll get you interviews, but it's your responsibility to turn those interviews into book sales.

As I said before, getting interviews is the "easy" part. Turning interviews into book sales is the hard part.

That's why I wrote this guide. I want to help you focus on the hard part that makes the biggest difference.

You can get all of the media coverage that you desire. But, if don't perform correctly, those opportunities will result in disappointment.

In case you're still dead-set on learning how to secure interviews, feel free to check out my online course called *How to Sell Books on a Shoestring Budget*. Visit: www.RobEagar.com/Shoestring-Course

There's a module within my course that explains step-by-step how to secure podcast interviews by yourself. This isn't an upsell. I only mention this resource if you're adamant on getting instruction for that part of the process.

But, I repeat...getting interviews is the EASY part. The way that you manage an interview is the real key to success.

Too many authors obsess about getting on the major shows, such as *Good Morning America, The Today Show, NPR,* or a big-time podcast. Yet, the competition to appear on those programs is fierce, which makes your overall chances to appear quite slim.

The wise approach is to pursue any level of media coverage that reaches the right readers for your book, regardless if it's large or small. Then, use those interviews to gain exposure, build your platform, and increase sales.

In this guide, I'm going to spell out how to use an interview to create book sales and grow your audience. Everything covered in this resource is applicable to authors of all genres, including fiction and nonfiction. Here's a look at the important goals you will learn how to achieve:

- How to prepare for an interview
- How to control an interview even with a weird host
- How to sell books during an interview
- How to track the results of an interview

Plus, I'll share a dirty little secret that the media industry doesn't want authors to know.

Everything in this guide applies to modern podcasts and social media channels as well as traditional radio and television appearances. Media technology may always change, but the principles for interview success remain the same.

If you're ready, let's lay the groundwork by learning how to properly prepare for an interview.

PART I

HOW TO PREPARE FOR AN INTERVIEW

1

WHY TEASING IS BETTER THAN TELLING

Ladies and gentlemen, may I have your attention?

This simple question sums up the primary goal of doing media interviews. Today, we live in the "attention economy," which means that business revolves around grabbing people's attention.

In other words, if you can hold someone's attention, you increase the ability to gain their trust and sell them a product.

In contrast, if you fail to gain someone's attention, you lose the opportunity to gain trust and sell a product.

There is no selling without attention. *AIDA*

Thus, preparing for an interview starts by learning how to command a listener's attention. But, this is where many authors shoot themselves in the foot.

Some authors mistakenly believe that giving an interview is a prime opportunity to tell the audience everything about their book. They see the microphone and think "class is now in session" with a captive audience. Nonfiction authors attempt to tell everyone everything that they know about their subject. Meanwhile, fiction authors tend to tell too many details about their novel and give away all of the suspense.

Two major problems occur when you tell the audience too much about your book.

First, your audience is never really captive. They don't have to listen to you if they don't feel interested. They can turn off the program, change the channel, pay attention to something else, or let their mind wander. It is your responsibility to keep the audience's attention riveted on you.

Second, most media interviews last less than 5 minutes, especially on radio and TV. That short span isn't nearly enough time to tell anyone much about your book.

Even if you appear on a podcast for 30 - 60 minutes, people don't want to endure listening to an author who drones on and on about every detail of their book.

Therefore, it's crucial to use a media interview to achieve this counterintuitive goal:

Pro tip:
Don't tell the audience about the book.
Tease the audience to want your book.

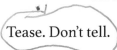

Tease. Don't tell.

Say it with me again: tease, don't tell.

At first glance, I know the word, "tease," may seem manipulative. You might think it's unethical to tease the audience or just shameless self-promotion.

I wrote this book to challenge your misconceptions and set the record straight. So, if you think I'm out of line, then let's consider the true ethics of giving an interview.

Imagine you've written a non-fiction book that helps parents communicate with their children. Or, maybe you wrote a fiction novel about a woman who overcomes a painful family tragedy. If you had an opportunity to discuss your book in the media, what would be the most ethical approach?

Would it be honorable to overwhelm your audience by rapidly attempting to tell listeners everything within your book in 10 minutes or less? Would you respect an author who tries to cram too many teaching points into the discussion? No, that approach only frustrates the audience with information overload.

Worse, most listeners won't remember what you say, because you inject too many topics to follow. Therefore, "telling" people about your book creates a cancellation effect whereby nobody learns anything. Thus, the best interview approach is to use the short time available to tease people's interest to get your book and read the complete message.

Tease...don't tell. It's ethical, and it works.

To be clear, teasing the audience doesn't mean that you avoid giving listeners helpful information. On the contrary, you still need to provide helpful nuggets of value or entertainment that is interesting. But, avoid trying to discuss your entire manuscript or delve too deeply into a novel's plot during an interview.

Tell the audience only what they NEED to know, not everything you know.

Most interviews fly by in an instant. So, use the brief opportunity to engage the audience, build their interest in your book, and motivate them to act. How do you do that quickly and effectively? I recommend this two-step strategy:

1. Develop your interview dialogue based on a few main points
2. Create attention-grabbing sound bites that listeners will remember

Let's look at each step in more detail.

HOW TO DEVELOP MAIN POINTS FOR AN INTERVIEW

Most interviews last for only a few minutes, so your objective is to quickly engage the audience, give enticing information, and lead listeners to purchase.

How do you decide what to tell and what to ignore? What information teases the most interest versus what information is a dull waste of time?

The average novel and nonfiction book contain too many particulars for the author to give a "Cliff-notes" review of every chapter. That's why you should only choose a few key points, just 2 – 4 specific items, that you want the audience to remember.

For instance, if you write nonfiction, it's important to begin an interview by establishing your expertise in order for listeners to feel like they can trust you. Share only the parts of your personal story that capture the audience's attention and boost your credibility. Present yourself as an interesting person who can relate to the problems that the audience faces.

Want to see a fantastic example of a nonfiction author mastering this dynamic?

Use the link below to watch a short video by author, Charles Duhigg, for his *New York Times* bestselling book, *The Power of Habit*:

https://www.youtube.com/watch?v=W1eYrhGeffc

Notice how Charles doesn't tell you everything about his book. In less than 3 minutes, he boils his entire book down to the most interesting points, such as:

- *Imagine having a bad habit you really want to change*
- *My habit led to gaining 8 pounds and my wife making pointed comments at me*
- *Habits start with a cue that creates a routine*
- *You can diagnose a habit and change it in any way that you want*
- *What habit do you want to change?*
- *Learn more at: ThePowerofHabit.com*

Charles didn't tell you everything about his book. Instead, he teased you to get a copy. You don't need to create a fancy video like Charles did. But, you do need to develop interesting main points that hold the listener's attention during an interview.

Novelists can also achieve this goal. For instance, one of my *New York Times* bestselling clients, Wanda Brunstetter, has sold over 12 million romance novels set in the Amish enclaves across America. She knows people are fascinated by the Amish lifestyle and the peaceful lives they pursue. She writes stories to capture those situations.

When Wanda conducts a media interview, she limits her discussion to the most fascinating points that people want to know, such as:

- *Why do the Amish choose such a primitive lifestyle?*
- *What is "wilding" and why do Amish kids do it?*
- *How do Amish families select marriage partners for their kids?*
- *How do Amish children interact with the world?*
- *Learn more and get free Amish recipes at:* *WandaBrunstetter.com*

As a novelist, Wanda doesn't reveal the ending of her stories during an author interview. Nor does she tell listeners too much information about the plot. Instead, she teases listeners by discussing the issues play into their curiosity. She uses her extensive knowledge of Amish culture to capture the audience's attention, hold their interest, and tease them to read her books.

A "talking point" is a fact, statement, or idea that you want listeners to remember after the interview is over. Don't waste precious time discussing non-essential background information or extraneous details about your book. You've only got a few minutes to connect with listeners. Keep the audience focused on the few spicy points that will hold their interest.

For instance, you could break down your interview into a few main points that provide an interesting statistic, a shocking or heartwarming personal story, answers to frequently asked questions, or a big problem in society that your book addresses.

I've appeared on dozens of podcasts, radio shows, and TV programs, and I never fly by the seat of my pants. Before any interview, I predetermine the topics that I know will tease listeners the most. Typically, I'll try to cover these three main points:

1. Share my personal story to gain credibility with the audience.
2. Provide one or two pieces of counterintuitive advice so that the audience thinks, "Wow, I've never heard that before. That guy sounds like an expert."
3. Discuss a popular trend in society and explain how my book can serve as a helpful resource for top-notch instruction.

Pro tip:
Write out your talking points on paper or type them into your smartphone and memorize the list before your interview.

In other words, don't "show up" for the interview. "Control" the interview.

When you discuss your book in public, you should know what to say beforehand and dictate the topics that are addressed. All of those details can be prearranged and practiced well before an interview starts.

Likewise, you should prepare for an interview by predetermining the topics you will mention. It's your book. It's your expertise. Thus, you should decide what is said.

By the way, if you're worried about how to control the flow of an interview or feel nervous about dealing with an antagonistic host, I'll provide answers to those issues later in this resource. Keep reading.

Will planning out your interview points make you sound canned? Only if you talk like a robot. Otherwise, organizing everything ahead of time will dramatically boost your confidence in front of the microphone and video camera. It's much better to be prepared and risk sounding canned than to "wing it" and blow a wonderful book-selling opportunity. Preparation gives you the right to feel confident.

If you conduct an interview and don't feel confident, it's because you didn't predetermine and practice the main talking points beforehand.

The good news is that preparation is within your complete control. Therefore, a successful interview is within your complete control.

CREATE QUESTIONS FOR YOUR OWN INTERVIEW

Once you've established the main points for your interview, the next step is to develop questions that will lead the host to ask you about those main points. It's like having someone lob you easy softballs to hit out of the park.

If you're new to the interviewing process, you might wonder, "Isn't the host supposed to come up with the questions?" That would seem plausible. But, in reality, most hosts are so busy that they don't have time to read your book and create clever questions.

Instead, the majority of media producers and podcast hosts are happy to follow a list of questions that you give them. They may throw in a few questions of their own or change the order of your questions to sound spontaneous. Generally, though, they will follow the roadmap that you provide.

This is good news, because it allows you to script most of the interview and make sure you touch on your main points. The key, however, is to make your interview questions sound natural and conversational.

For instance, don't write, "Question #1 – Why did you write your book?" or "Question #2 – What is your book about?" That would make the host sound like an inhuman robot, which they won't appreciate.

Instead, phrase your questions in a manner that sounds normal during a typical conversation. In addition, don't be afraid to make your questions provocative or controversial. You want people to stay glued to the interview instead of tuning you out. For example, you could write opening questions, such as:

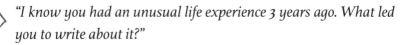

"I know you had an unusual life experience 3 years ago. What led you to write about it?"

"You believe most people look at their relationship problems from the wrong angle. What do you mean by that?"

"If art imitates life, how does your novel connect with the current issues in our culture?

Most media programs will let you script the interview by sending questions to them ahead of time.

Pro tip:
Create questions that make it easy to talk about your main points and the best parts of your book. Send those questions to the interview host beforehand.

Your interview will only be as good as the script that you prepare.

Don't worry, you won't sound like a robot.

Scripting a conversation happens in every other artistic endeavor. All actors rehearse and deliver scripted lines. All musicians sing pre-scripted lyrics. But, they present their lines in a way that is natural, because they practice beforehand and internalize the content.

Professional actors know that once you memorize your lines, you actually come alive on camera. The more embedded the words are in your brain, the more fun you can have saying them. Likewise, copy your artistic brethren and script your media interview for success.

Is it okay to use the same questions for every interview that you give? Absolutely.

Very few podcasts, radio programs, or TV shows have the exact same audience. That means you are always talking to new people who've never heard you before.

Thus, there is no need add unnecessary work to your already busy schedule. Use the same interview questions over and over. Say the same things over and over. People won't tire of hearing an author discuss interesting topics again - as long as they are memorable.

But, how do you create interview dialogue that is intriguing? Find the secret in the next chapter.

4

ANSWER QUESTIONS WITH A SOUND BITE

Remember how I blew my big national interview on *The CBS Early Show*? That wasn't my first media mistake. Before that blunder, I wasted other opportunities to promote my book on radio and television.

When I initially conducted author interviews, I made the rookie mistake of being a "motor mouth." Put candidly, I talked too much, gave too many uninteresting details, and bored the audience with long, drawn-out dialogue. Sometimes, I would take over two minutes to answer a question and barely take a breath in the process. The host could hardly get a word in edgewise.

Worse, I would attempt to wrap up my long-winded answers with a clever statement at the end. By that time, however, the audience had lost interest and tuned me out. To them, listening to me was like reading a long newspaper article with no headlines or section breaks. They needed something to grab their attention when I answered questions and hold their interest throughout the interview.

After fumbling through several radio appearances and watching more experienced authors amaze their audiences, I realized a better approach was necessary. I needed to talk less and speak in a more engaging manner. I needed to employ the power of sound bites.

> A "sound bite" is a memorable statement that grabs the listener's attention and summarizes your answer to an interview question.

When used correctly, a "sound bite" will stick in a listener's mind long after your interview is over. Staying in the listener's memory is crucial to selling more books.

In addition, using sound bites helps condense your interview answers to prevent being long-winded. It's always better to talk less and leave the audience wanting more, rather than to talk too long and bore the listener.

Pro Tip:
Before an interview, practice answering each of your pre-created questions in 60 seconds or less.

The best way to avoid motor-mouth syndrome is rehearse answering your questions quickly and concisely. Get a timer or use the stopwatch app on your smartphone. Put the timer in front of you, hit start, then practice saying your answers out loud in 60 seconds or less.

I don't mean that you should talk faster. Instead, cut out the fluff. Identify the unnecessary details and force yourself to only say what the audience needs to hear in less than a minute.

Want to become an interview ninja? Try this exercise. Record yourself with a videocamera or smartphone practicing your answers out loud in 60 seconds or less. Then, listen to the recording with a critical ear. Even better, let somebody else listen and critique your performance.

Sure, it can be terrifying to hear yourself stumbling through interview answers for the first time. But, that is how you get better and improve your skills. When you examine your practice session, ask yourself the following questions:

- Am I talking at a relaxed pace or talking too fast?
- Can I answer each question in 60 seconds or less?
- Do I sound interesting or boring?
- Is the energy in my voice exciting or listless?

It's always better to answer questions succinctly and let the host encourage you to talk more, rather than talk too much and lose the audience's interest. Once you're able to answer interview questions concisely, then you have the freedom to elaborate if the opportunity arises. Above all, you maintain control over the conversation.

Unfortunately, too many authors make the mistake of being long-winded with their answers and never learn to talk concisely. Don't make this mistake. Otherwise, you risk losing the audience's interest, losing your credibility, and losing book sales. Sound bites help you avoid this problem.

Think about sound bites like a news editor uses attention-grabbing headlines to introduce articles. Without headlines, nobody would read the newspaper or scan their online news feeds. A headline is critical to grabbing the reader's interest and inviting them into the article. It's wise to use the same approach when answering media interview questions.

Each time an interviewer asks you a question, begin your answer with a short sound bite that draws the audience's attention. It's like giving the listener a headline to solidify their interest. This approach also helps keep your audience listening during the rest of your answer.

Logic makes people think, but emotion makes them act. Therefore, a good sound bite should generate emotion in your listeners, such as laughter, curiosity, or even anger. When people feel a deeper interest in you and your book, they are more likely to purchase.

Plus, some people will be listening to your interview while driving in their car, going for a walk, or working out at the gym. There are easy alternatives that can distract their attention. Likewise, it may be long time before they are in a position to purchase your book online or visit a bookstore. Thus, if you use sound bites that stick in people's minds, you increase the probability that they will act later.

Let's look at how sound bites can be used for fiction and nonfiction situations.

If you write fiction, a sound bite can relate to the over-arching aspect of your novel. For instance, if a media host asks why you wrote your book, you could answer with a concise memorable reply, such as:

I wrote my novel because...

What if the first astronaut to visit Mars realizes he'll be the first to die there?

What if you had to choose between killing your wife to save your daughter?

What if a woman had led the civil rights movement instead of Martin Luther King?

Intelligent machines have calculated that the best source of energy...is humans.

A man was grieving over his dead girlfriend...until she reappeared.

Notice how each question and statement piques your interest and makes you want to know more. That's the power of a sound bite. Just like a newspaper headline, they act as a perfect tool to gain the listener's attention.

If you write nonfiction, a sound bite can utilize counterintuitive teaching points or little-known statistics that grab the listener's interest, such as:

I wrote my book to show the world...

What if your sex life can get hotter with age?

Anyone can be debt-free in 12 months, no matter how much you owe.

Did you know that you can train your brain to win?

Amazon rainforest land equal to 31 million football fields disappears each year.

Any people-pleaser can learn how to say "No" without feeling guilty.

These attention-grabbing sound bites make you want to know more. You want to find out what else the author has to say. In essence, you're harnessing the power of curiosity to maintain control over the listener's interest.

Not sure how to create sound bites based on your book? Try these ideas:

1. Go through your manuscript and look at the call out quotes that you or your publisher highlighted within the text. Those standout quotes might be good candidates for sound bites.

2. Review the feedback about your book from your beta readers, focus groups, or launch team members. Were there any quotes or excerpts that they found especially memorable?

3. Are there any clever statements or sound bite ideas you can pull from your book description or back cover copy?

Once you identify content from your book that is noteworthy, use that material to develop a sound bite for every potential question you could be asked. Experienced media professionals always prepare ahead of time. They never leave anything to chance.

Remember, you get to script your interview beforehand. Use that power to your advantage. Create sound bites and be ready to wield them.

By the way, if you don't know how to create effective sound bites or book hooks that grab people's interest, I've got a special gift for you. Go to Amazon and get a free copy of my short e-book called, **Mastering Book Hooks for Authors.**

http://getbook.at/MasterBookHooks

Over 10,000 authors have downloaded this free resource. I'm confident that it will help you improve your attention-grabbing game.

5

ACT LIKE AN EQUAL TO THE HOST

Even though you can script your interview beforehand doesn't mean everything will be easy. There can be other factors that work against you, such as a short time limit, a bossy or antagonistic host, or other guests on the program competing for attention. But, there is another factor that can wreak the most havoc on your interview – fear within your mind.

When you're new to the media world, it can be nerve-wracking to sit in front of a microphone. Likewise, it's easy to feel awestruck about sitting on a sound stage surrounded by technical people, bright lights, and expensive equipment. That sense of awe can make you feel inferior to the host. You might even think, "Aw shucks, I'm just a yokel author from the country who doesn't belong here."

If you carry an inferior or anxious mindset into your interview, I can guarantee what will happen – the audience will sense your fear.

[B sure]

If you come across as uncomfortable, guess what? The host and the audience will feel uncomfortable. Worse, listeners won't buy your book when they feel uncomfortable.

How do you overcome interview anxiety? The solution begins before you show up.

Before you ever agree to do a media interview, you must get over your awe of the media. How do you overcome awe of something or someone else?

Act like an equal.

I'm dead serious. You are an equal to any media producer, podcast owner, and television host. You aren't better than them. But, they aren't better than you. You are equal peers entering into a mutually beneficial situation.

Purposefully fight any kind of hayseed mentality that makes you think, "Look, Mom! I'm on TV!" or "Wow, I'm on a big-time podcast!" *Leverage is God-ordained just is now*

Here's why a mindset of equality is critical to a successful interview. If you classify yourself as someone who doesn't deserve to be in front of an audience, the host and listeners will pick up on your insecurity.

When a host senses that your anxious, then he or she is put in a difficult position of trying to carry you through an unpleasant conversation, which is an annoying burden on their end. Likewise, most audience listeners will change the channel or tune out a guest who acts insecure. It's no fun to watch someone fail on live radio or TV.

Therefore, you must convince yourself that you BELONG

on radio, TV, and podcasts before you can convince other people.

Pro tip:
The first sale is always to yourself. Rather than act inferior, view yourself as someone who is equal to the host and the audience.

Acting like an equal means interacting with your interview host as a peer. He or she isn't better than you. Instead, you are equals, which means you can respectfully disagree, ask for any needed cooperation, and expect professional treatment from one another.

The media industry needs authors just as much as authors need exposure for their books. Radio, TV, and podcast programs cannot exist without lively guests to keep each episode fresh and entertaining. Otherwise, their ratings would fall and the show would be canceled. As an author, you are a valuable asset.

Likewise, you need a way to promote your book to a large group of people. Without the media, it would be harder to reach thousands of readers in a short period of time. Consequently, you need each other as equal partners to make something good happen. Thus, don't cower like a beggar who's simply glad to be giving an interview. Conduct yourself like someone who deserves to be in front of the microphone.

Besides acting like equals, another way to overcome fear of the media is to prepare like a professional. This type of preparation includes creating effective questions, sending them ahead of time to the host, and practicing answers to any oddball topics that might arise. You don't need to prepare for every eventuality. But, you want to have a working knowledge of your book and any current headlines related to your subject matter so that you're ready to offer insightful answers.

This may sound corny, but here's how I personally overcame my fear of the media and started giving standout interviews.

Days before an interview, I used to sit in my office and practice saying my sound bites and interview answers out loud. Sometimes, I would ask my wife to pretend like she was the host and ask me questions. In addition, I'd use a timer to rehearse how long it took to recite my main points and share personal story. I practiced weaving my main points into the discussion and made any adjustments until I could answer any question in less than 60 seconds.

By the time my interview day arrived, I was brimming with confidence. I no longer feared the bright lights in my face. I felt like a relaxed pro who was excited to share my book with the world.

On several occasions, I gave such a good interview that the program director immediately asked if I would be willing to come back on the show in the future. That type of request is when you know the media industry views you as a valuable asset.

Remember that some of your interviews may be recorded live. So, you can't afford to stumble through your answers and hope someone will edit your mistakes. When you're on live radio or TV, you only get one shot to do it right.

In summary, act like an equal with the media and never attempt to fly by the seat of your pants. Only amateurs "wing it," because they're lazy and inconsiderate of the audience. If you take a careless attitude towards an interview, your audience will respond with a careless attitude toward your book.

You and your book deserve better than that.

6

HOW TO CONTROL AN INTERVIEW CONVERSATION

How do you know if you're a true interview pro? A good way to gauge your media prowess is your ability to steer the conversation to only the topics that you want to discuss.

Hear me clearly – just because the host asks you a question does NOT mean that you must answer it.

Of course, it's polite to respond to someone's question. But, if the host starts going down a verbal rabbit trail, you are NOT obligated to follow and waste time away from talking about your main points.

Occasionally, you may interact with a host who is condescending or openly disagrees with your opinions. Don't let him or her bully you. Instead, sidestep the argument and redirect the question to a subject that you want to discuss.

Imagine conducting an interview like driving a car. The host is in the passenger seat asking the questions, but you're in the driver's seat steering the direction of the conversation.

For example, here are three responses you can say when a host asks an antagonistic or irrelevant question:

"Yes, that's an interesting issue. But, I've found that an even bigger issue is..."

"I'll be glad to answer that question. But, first, let me say something about..."

"You bring up a good question. But, before I leave, I really want to emphasize this point to the listeners..."

Remember, you're the expert, not the host. Therefore, it makes sense for you to control the discussion about your book, rather than the host who has never read it.

Pro tip:
Watch how politicians and executives carefully steer any
interview discussion to their main points.

The next time you're channel-surfing on TV, tune-in to CNN or FOX News. When an interview segment occurs, notice how politicians or corporate executives try to control the interview discussion. These people can take almost any question, negative or positive, and cleverly steer the answer to the main point that they want to make.

Yes, you might find their behavior annoying, because politicians rarely say anything with much substance. But, they have an incredible ability to stay focused on their agenda, which is your same goal as an author. Plus, you're better than a politician, because you've got something positive to discuss. With a little practice, you can develop a similar ability to always steer an irrelevant question back to your book.

Before I conclude this topic, let me clarify that I'm not advocating manipulation or impolite behavior on the air. You should always act professional. However, you must realize that securing national media exposure for your book is difficult. Never take it lightly. You probably won't get a second chance to be on the program again.

If you fumble an interview because you were ill-prepared or were intimidated by the situation, then it's a disservice to your audience, yourself, and your book sales.

Only you can make an interview successful. Now you know how.

7

ALWAYS SMILE FOR THE CAMERA

At the beginning of this resource, I shared the story of getting interviewed on the *CBS Early Show*. Up until that time, I had only done a couple of small-time interviews that only reached a handful of listeners. Thus, right after the *Early Show* producer contacted me, my jubilation quickly turned to anxiety. I had never experienced being in front of an audience of millions.

Regretfully, I approached the opportunity like an amateur and never realized the need to create a plan for success. Instead, I worried about what I would look like on camera. At least my wife had the presence of mind to suggest we take a few practice runs. So, I sat in my office one afternoon while she lobbed practice questions at me.

During our mock rehearsal, however, my wife noticed something strange. She said, "You don't look relaxed when you answer the questions. Instead, you look defensive and anxious."

I responded, "What do you mean? I feel confident."

We argued back and forth until she said something that changed my perspective, "Go look at yourself in the mirror."

Lo and behold, she was right.

We walked into the bathroom and conducted another practice round. When I watched myself answer her questions in the mirror, I looked awful. (You can also use your smartphone or tablet device to record and playback a practice interview.) I had no idea that the image I portrayed appeared so negative.

Without the mirror, I thought I had looked fine. Yet, in reality, my face looked dour, and I appeared uncomfortable. That's when I learned the Golden Rule for video interviews.

Pro tip:
When you appear on camera, smile constantly. Keep smiling...
even if it hurts.

I don't care if your cheeks cramp up or the host insults you. Never stop smiling while the camera is running. You've probably heard the phrase, "The camera adds 10 pounds." I believe that smiling on camera adds 10 times to your credibility, which helps increase your audience engagement.

Here's an example to explain what I mean. Years ago, I watched an interview on *60 Minutes* with a Wal-Mart executive who used smiling to her advantage. This executive was defending her company's position in a lawsuit over the location of a new store. The reporter from *60 Minutes* kept grilling her with harsh, accusatory questions. Yet, during the entire interview, this Wal-Mart official never stopped smiling. She sat with a pleasant demeanor, patiently answered questions, and never once looked perturbed. Even if viewers disagreed with her position, she came across as credible and professional. I found myself liking who she seemed to be as a person. It was a strange interview to witness, but that scene reinforced the power of smiling on camera.

Likewise, always smile on camera during your author interview. Oddly enough, smiling can even help improve your podcast and radio interviews as well. Even though people may not be able to see you, your smiling demeanor will translate into what they hear.

Hopefully, you'll never be questioned by a hard-hitting reporter from *60 Minutes*. But, if it happens, be ready to hold your own with a smile.

PART II

HOW TO SELL BOOKS DURING AN INTERVIEW

So far, I've explained how to prepare for an interview and control the conversation. But, I know you're wondering, "Rob, how do I actually sell books during an interview?"

The whole goal of doing media appearances is to sell books. If an interview doesn't help move copies, then what's the point? Let's dive into this objective.

Never forget that answering questions from a host and enticing listeners to purchase are two completely different issues. They also require separate skills.

Many authors find it nerve-racking to promote a book during a podcast, radio, or television appearance. Nobody wants to come across as a sleazy used-car salesman hocking a product.

Thus, the real question is: How do you lead audience listeners to buy your book in a tasteful manner?

The simple answer is to give such an engaging interview that listeners can't help but want a copy of your book. Of course, that's easier said than done. Plus, there are many variables that are difficult to manage, such as the behavior of the host, the timing of the interview broadcast, or competing for airtime with other guests.

Fortunately, there are two ways to encourage people to purchase in a manner that gives you control over the process. One technique uses a short-term approach to sell books quickly. The other technique uses a longer-term approach to sell books in the future. Both techniques are equally effective:

1. Make your book seem scarce (short-term approach)

2. Entice people to join your email list (long-term approach)

Let's examine each technique in more detail.

8

MAKE YOUR BOOK SEEM SCARCE – EVEN IF IT'S NOT

When you conduct a media interview, you hope people will like what you say and buy your book. But, there's an unseen problem that can prevent listeners from making a purchase. In today's modern publishing industry, the dominance of online retailers and existence of e-books means something unique: books are never scarce.

Essentially, there is an unlimited supply of books available for readers to purchase. But, that fact isn't necessarily good news. There's a major downside associated with this reality:

If books are always available online,
then buyers can always wait.

Since your book is always available, you face a constant roadblock that can hinder the act of purchasing. This road-block is a lack of urgency. Without urgency, people who listen to your interview can indefinitely postpone their decision to purchase.

The audience may love what they hear you say on a podcast, radio show, or TV program. But, their enthusiasm can be easily misdirected or distracted by all of the other busy occurrences in a normal daily life, such as dealing with pressures at work, caring for the kids, managing family issues, getting dinner ready, meeting with friends, etc.

This reality creates a dynamic where a lot of interview listeners will think to themselves:

I'm busy today, I'll get that author's book next week...

I'll get that author's book next time I'm in a bookstore...

I'll get that author's book as a gift for so-and-so next month...

I'll get that author's book after next year's budget is approved...

Notice how easy it is for people to delay buying your book. In their minds, they have a good reason to wait until a later date. But, this reveals the major problem:

> *The vast majority of people who wait to purchase*
> *will never buy your book in the future.*

Delaying a purchase means the odds of an actual purchase are slim-to-none. This explains why most authors fail to sell many books after a media interview. They are completely unprepared for the delayed response that the audience will naturally invoke.

What's a poor author to do in this situation? There is hope, my creative comrades!

Give listeners a compelling reason to avoid delaying the purchase. Entice them to buy quickly.

Yes, you can do this. It works. It's ethical. And, I'm giving you permission to do it.

When a product is always available, you must overcome people's apathy to buy by creating a sense of urgency in their minds. You do this by heightening the "fear of missing out" (also known as FOMO). When you develop the fear of missing out, you move people from delaying the purchase to wanting to buy. It's not manipulation, it's positive psychology.

If you promote your book without creating a sense of FOMO, an analogy would be like letting someone else drive your car. You never want that to happen. You should always want to drive your own car. In the case of your book, a lack of FOMO during an interview is tantamount to letting the listening audience drive the decision to purchase, rather than you driving that decision.

In contrast, when you create a sense of FOMO, you manage the steering wheel and drive the car. You always want to be in control of the sales process. If you market your book using a willy-nilly, hope-and-pray approach, then good luck selling many books.

Believe me, I learned this lesson the hard way. For several years, I did media appearances with measly results. Nothing worked, no matter how hard I tried to be likable during the interview.

Fortunately, I ran across a book called *Launch* by Jeff Walker. Jeff's book hit #1 on the *New York Times* bestseller list, and he is known as the king of selling products online. As I read Jeff's book, I came across this interesting quote:

To create a well-executed launch, you absolutely need to build scarcity into that launch. There has to be some negative consequence if people don't take action and buy before the end of the launch, such as the price might go up. If you make sure there's always some scarcity built into your launch, it will take your results to a completely different level.

Jeff's comment about "scarcity" set off a light bulb in my mind. Scarcity is the key to creating the fear of missing out. If people think something good is about to disappear, they are more motivated to act.

However, there's still a problem. Since almost every book can be purchased on Amazon at any time, then books are never scarce. Thus, people can still postpone their purchase to a later time. How do you overcome this inertia?

Pro tip:
Create something that is scarce and combine it with your book to generate a sense of urgency.

Here's an amazing secret that I urge you to never forget. Any author can artificially manufacture scarcity for a book at any time. Your book may not be scarce, but you can create an exclusive item or a special offer that people would really want. Then, make that item disappear within a limited time, such as:

- Discounted price
- Chance to meet the author
- Entry into a private Q&A session
- Access to exclusive teaching
- Lost chapters or bonus content
- Sweepstakes to win prizes
- Fiction: Exclusive novella or short story

This technique creates what I like to call "artificial scarcity." You artificially make your book seem scarce, even though it isn't. Now you have greater control over people's urge to purchase.

As you conduct an author interview, tell listeners about your scarce "bonus" item or the "special offer" that will soon vanish. Pause at the beginning and end of your interview to tell listeners something like the following:

"I'm grateful to be on this program, so I put together a very special offer for everyone listening!

If you buy a copy of my book by this date _____, I will give you this exclusive bonus 10mm. But, you must act before it disappears. Get the details on my website at HTC." hopeacope.com

This appeal is easy to insert into an interview, especially if you're running a unique incentive during a book launch or giving interviews during an author tour. For best results, mention this "scarce" offer at least two times during your interview. In addition, it's good to mention a specific deadline to heighten the urgency, such as:

Only good for the next 48 hours... [handwritten: 24 48 hours / tonight!]

Bonuses disappear at the end of this week... [handwritten: tonight!]

The offer ends on this date: [handwritten: tonight (do it now!) first 40 X]

When I manage book launches for my top clients, we develop bonus content ahead of time or set up an exclusive author access that will only be available for a limited period. Then, we give access to those bonuses after a customer completes the purchase and follows these simple steps:

Step 1 – Purchase the author's book at any retailer

Step 2 – Take a picture of the store receipt or online order

Step 3 – Go to the author's webpage for the book

Step 4 – Fill out a short form with contact info

Step 5 – Upload a picture of the order receipt

Step 6 – Receive instructions on the "thank-you page" to claim the bonuses

This process can be automated so that no one has to monitor the system, which saves time. Or, you can have the individual customer requests go to someone on your author team who verifies that each purchase is legitimate. Once they deem the purchase is authentic, then they respond by email with a link to access the bonuses.

You can decide which option is right for you. Creating artificial scarcity makes it easy to "turn on" and "turn off" the urgency to buy without adding extra expenses or labor.

What if you're not in the middle of a new book launch? You can still create artificial scarcity for a backlist book by offering an incentive and telling listeners that it will soon disappear. Use the same process that I just described to manage delivery of your incentive when readers provide their purchase receipts.

When you attach an enticing incentive to your book that will soon vanish, you heighten people's desire to buy your book. Now, you are in control of the sales process.

To recap, if you want to drive book sales during an author interview, you have two options. First, you must be incredibly famous, uniquely charismatic, and write a rare one-of-a-kind book. Obviously, most authors don't possess those characteristics. Therefore, the second option can be employed, which is to spur book sales by creating artificial scarcity.

Never let your book sales be left to chance or subject to the listener's apathy. Take charge of your author interview and lead listeners to purchase by offering something attractive that will soon disappear.

9

OFFER INCENTIVES TO BUILD YOUR EMAIL LIST

Creating artificial scarcity is a short-term technique that can drive book sales during a media interview. But, there is a long-term approach that can be just as effective. And, when I say, "long-term," I don't mean years later – that's too long. Instead, I mean only a few days, weeks, or months later.

Let's be realistic. The majority of people who listen to your interview aren't going to immediately buy your book, even if you incentivize them with artificial scarcity. That's normal for most authors, including the celebrities.

But, there's another option you can employ to produce a positive result. Use the media interview to build your author email list. If you can't win the immediate book sale, then win the long-term opportunity to build your email list and market your books repeatedly to people in the future. The outcome can be just as beneficial.

Once someone is on your email list, you receive unlimited ability to promote your book to that person in the future, such as next week or next month. The easiest way to increase sales is to generate purchases from your personal followers.

If you never build your email list, then you remain at a marketing disadvantage. Here's a true story to prove my point.

One of my former consulting clients is Dr. Harville Hendrix. He has the unique distinction of being one of the most popular guests to ever appear on *The Oprah Winfrey Show.* Throughout the late-1990's and early-2000's, Dr. Hendrix was interviewed by Oprah over 15 times!

Imagine being on national television viewed by millions of people while Oprah is singing your praises in front of a live studio audience. Dr. Hendrix enjoyed the equivalence of media paradise. Of course, his book became a bestseller and he gained notoriety. But, the after-effects of appearing on Oprah's program didn't have a happy ending.

Once his interviews on *The Oprah Winfrey Show* were over, Dr. Hendrix noticed that his book sales began to decline. He assumed that being on national TV over 15 times would keep him famous and maintain a bestseller status. But, his sales continued to lessen.

When Dr. Hendrix and I first met, I asked him, "How did you use *The Oprah Winfrey Show* to build your own tribe of followers?"

"I never thought about it that way," he replied. "I was just happy to be in front of Oprah's huge audience."

"Appearing on Oprah was good for your short-term success, but it created a long-term problem," I responded. "When you lost access to Oprah's audience, then you had no audience of your own to create future book sales. Instead, you now have to start over from scratch."

"Oh my gosh!" he exclaimed as the harsh reality set in. "You're right. If I had taken steps to build my own audience while I was being interviewed on Oprah, I would have it much easier today."

I'll never forget what he said next, "I really wish I'd known about your media strategy before I ever went on *Oprah*."

I went on to help Dr. Hendrix build his email list using other methods. But, he missed a golden opportunity to grow his audience while appearing on the most popular daytime TV show in America.

That's why I wrote this guide. I don't want you to make the same mistake. You can use any media interview to grow your email list – and you can look like a hero while you do it. Here's how.

Before you hire a publicity firm or line up interviews on your own, take time to develop 2 – 3 pieces of "bonus content" that you can offer as incentives for people to join your email list. For example, you could create any of the following items as enticing bait:

.   .   .

Email Signup Incentive Ideas for Nonfiction Authors:

- Create a concise e-book packed with helpful advice
- "Lost chapters" or bonus teaching not in your book
- 7-day or 30-day challenge using content from book
- Short video course based on material in your book
- Audio exercise based on instruction in your book

Email Signup Incentive Ideas for Fiction Authors:

- Offer a short story or standalone novella
- Write a prequel or sequel related to your novel
- Assemble a collection of short stories
- Create a "sampler" with a few chapters from each of your novels

You can offer any of these ideas as an effective enticement to attract email signups. But, you'll get even better results when you package a few incentives together into an irresistible package. Doing so makes you seem like a generous-minded individual who wants to give people lots of free content.

Then, when you conduct an interview, you're able to happily say, "I've got several amazing gifts that I'd like to give everyone listening for free. Just go to my website at ___, join my email list, and claim your gifts today, which include these items..."

Notice how it's easier to get people to claim your free gifts than ask them to buy your book. You're also likely to get more listeners to respond to your free offer. Once they join your email list, you can remind them about buying your book as much as you want. So, you can still close the sale within a short timeframe. It's like having your cake and getting to eat it, too.

Pro tip:
Mention your email signup offer at least twice during an interview.

Once is rarely enough, because many people may not listen to your entire interview. Or, they'll need reminding due to distractions around them.

For instance, work your incentive offer into one of your interview answers to make sure people hear about the opportunity. Then, mention your "free gifts" again at the end of your interview before wrapping up. Tell listeners to go to your author website to receive your free gift.

When listeners visit your website, make sure it's easy for them to see the free offer on your home page. If they arrive to your site and can't easily see your gifts, then you'll look like someone pulling a sleazy bait-and-switch maneuver.

For example, create a signup box on your website home page that says:

Sign-up for my email newsletter and get these free gifts: (insert the name of your freebie).

Once people fill out the signup form, you can deliver your incentive on the "thank you" page or have it automatically sent as a "welcome email" for joining your list.

By now, you might be thinking, "Why go through all of this trouble to get email signups?"

Well, it would be nice if everyone listening to your interview rushed to their local bookstore and bought a book. But, that's not going to happen.

However, if you motivate people to join your email list, then you increase the odds that they might buy a book in the future. Take the long-term view and use interviews to build your own audience. I have multiple clients who built their email lists to over 100,000 subscribers. At that level, they have amazing control to dictate their own success.

Once your personal audience gets large enough, you may never need to do media interviews again.

Just so you're aware, I teach advanced tactics to build a bigger email list and drive more sales in my book, *The Author's Guide to Email Marketing*. I encourage you to read that resource as a supplement to everything you learn in this guide. For details, visit:

http://getbook.at/AuthorEmailMarketing

10

THE MEDIA INDUSTRY'S DIRTY LITTLE SECRET

Did you know there's a dirty little secret that the media industry wants to keep hidden from authors?

Some radio programs and TV shows do NOT want you to mention your author website during an interview.

In fact, some hosts will refuse to say your website out loud or show it on the TV screen. Seems unfair, right?

In many cases, authors go out of their way, sometimes traveling at their own expense, to appear on a media program. That means a lot of shows are get their guests for free. When an author appears on a program for free, you would think the least they could do in return is tell the audience how to find the author online.

But, they rarely extend this courtesy – and they do it on purpose. This behavior is rude, because it means listeners will have to take more steps to find you online or locate information about your book. The more steps that listeners have to take, the less likely they are to act. Therefore, you wind up giving an interview that yields very few book sales, just because the media industry acts as a stumbling block.

If your name is hard to spell or your book title is hard to remember, then you're already at a disadvantage if the media doesn't display a link to your website.

Here's the rationale behind the media industry's ludicrous position. Some programs make a lot of money by charging for advertising space on their website, TV show ads, or podcast episodes. If they maximize visits to their websites, then they can charge more money for advertising space.

Therefore, many media outlets will refuse to mention your website on the air or provide a link to your book in their online show notes. That's because they don't want their audience to leave their website and go visit your site or one of the book retailers. Less traffic for them means less advertising revenue.

Fortunately, there is a clever way to get around this problem and look like a hero.

Remember the free incentives that I described in the previous section to build your email list? Those incentives can be used an "ace up your sleeve" to get around the media's dirty little secret.

Pro tip:
Mention your free incentive offer as a way to inject your website address into any interview conversation.

When you offer something for free as a helpful resource, you come across looking like the generous good guy.

Therefore, it's hard for the host to prevent you from talking about your website during the interview. There's no way a host will say, "Sorry, you can't mention your website or free offer to our listening audience." That would create a PR disaster for the host and make him or her look selfish.

They might be frustrated that you outfoxed them and took control of the interview, but that's their problem. Your problem is making sure the interview helps grow your audience and sell more books.

Therefore, don't be afraid to take charge of an interview. Be wise to the media industry's dirty little secret. Prevent selfish hosts from hurting your book sales by proactively mentioning your website where the audience can get your generous free gifts.

11

HOW TO TRACK RESULTS FROM YOUR INTERVIEW

The obvious goal of any media interview is to sell books. However, it's not always easy to monitor results in real-time. Thus, it can feel like you're flying blind.

If you self-publish using Amazon's KDP platform, you're able to track book sales via Amazon on a daily basis. So, you're able to see if an interview helps move the sales needle within a 24-hour basis.

However, if you're a traditionally-published author or self-published writer using a third-party company, tracking results isn't so easy. It could take days or weeks to get recent sales figures from your publisher. Therefore, you may not know if an interview helped created sales until it's too late to determine.

If you're in that situation, there are secondary statistics that you can track. For example, check your book's Amazon sales ranking before and after your interview goes live. If you see a marked improvement over 24 hours, you can assume that your interview had a positive impact.

You could also track how many people visited your website before and after an interview. If you have a Google account, you can use Google Analytics to access your website statistics for free.

If you offer free incentives to build your email list like I suggest, you can track how many signups you acquire within 24 – 72 hours after your interview. For example, if you receive 100 more signups than normal over that time period, that's a good indication that activity was a result of your interview.

If you secure a major appearance on a national-level TV program, let your publisher know ahead of time. They will be equally excited to see if the appearance moves the needle. Ask your publisher to monitor their sales figures and provide you with a sales update within a few days after your interview. They can usually do this by email with a quick turnaround.

Finally, if you happen to sell books directly from your author website, you can also examine the success of your interview by tracking the amount of orders placed within 24 – 72 hours afterwards. However, be aware that the vast majority of readers prefer to buy books from their favorite retailers who offer low prices and fast shipping, rather than purchase from an author's website.

Next, let's learn how to properly prepare for an interview.

12

INTERVIEW PREPARATION CHECKLIST

Practicing before an interview gives you the right to feel confident during an interview. Never attempt to "wing it" or cram at the last minute. Instead, use the checklist below to plan ahead for interview success:

One month before your interview:

- Set up enticing incentives on your website to build your author email list
- Create 5 – 10 questions that lead into your main discussion points
- Create answers for your questions that start with a memorable sound bite like _____
- Determine the most interesting or jaw-dropping personal stories you can share with the audience
- Practice answering each interview question in less than 60 seconds

app. for w.shops/ talks, sems? too. & p.casts

scary?!

One week before your interview:

- Send your interview questions ahead of time to the program host or producer
- Memorize your main points and sound bites for each interview question
- Practice your entire interview at least 3 times by answering every interview question with sound bites in less than 60 seconds
- If you'll be conducting a video interview, practice answering questions in front of a mirror or record yourself using a camera or smartphone
- Pick an outfit to wear on camera that makes you look professional and confident

The day before your interview:

- Contact the host to confirm your interview time and provide a cellphone number in case any technical problems occur
- Practice answering every interview question with sound bites in less than 60 seconds
- Practice reminding listeners about your free incentives to join your author email list
- Go to bed early and get a good night's sleep

See the next section for helpful tips during the day of your interview...

13

HELPFUL TIPS FOR THE DAY OF YOUR INTERVIEW

Let's imagine the big day for your interview has arrived. Here are some tips to help you remain composed, relaxed, and comfortable:

1. Print out your pre-planned interview questions along with the accompanying sound bites.

Keep this piece of paper in front of you during a podcast or radio interview. The host won't mind if you have a cheat sheet, and the listening audience will never know. It's best to memorize the information beforehand. But, you can use the paper printout as a "safety net" to calm your nerves during an interview and stay on track if you forget a particular point.

2. On your cheat sheet, write down the host's name and the program's title.

This step will help avoid an awkward moment in case you suddenly forget your interviewer's name. I learned this lesson the hard way when I did three different interviews back-to-back in one day and got one of the hosts' names mixed up...it wasn't pretty.

3. Keep a glass or bottle of water nearby.

Be prepared in case your mouth gets dry or you start to cough. There's no worse feeling than getting nervous in front of the microphone and leaving yourself stranded without any water. Always have water on hand.

4. Remove all potential background noise distractions.

If you're conducting an interview by phone or video from your home or office, remove any potential audio distractions, such as background noise from barking pets, crying babies, call waiting features, text chimes on your smartphone, or audible email notifications on your computer. Otherwise, your interview may get repeatedly interrupted by annoying sounds that make you look like an amateur.

5. Never say "my book," instead say the main title.

This may sound like a no-brainer, but never say "my book" during an interview. It's a classic mistake that too many authors repeatedly make. Whenever you conduct an interview, always say the full title of your book (you can skip the subtitle). If your book happens to have a long title, then mention a condensed version. But, never say "my book."

People usually need to hear your specific book title at least 3 – 4 times before they can remember it. Moreover, you can't expect everyone to listen to your entire interview. If you don't repeat your book title several times, most people won't remember it. Say your title a few times during the interview to help it stick in the listeners' minds.

6. Bring a copy of your book to the interview

Always bring a copy of your book to every interview, especially any video interview. That way, you can give a copy for the host to display on camera or hold up a copy for the audience to see. Also, you might get a chance to read directly from your book, which can convince more viewers to purchase.

7. Don't forget to mention your email signup offer.

Use your interview to do more than just sell books. It's a great opportunity to build your author email list. At the beginning and end of your interview, be sure to mention any free signup incentives that you're offering. People won't join your email list unless they hear you give them an enticing reason to do so.

8. Strive for success – not perfection.

It's okay if you forget part of an answer or get flustered in the moment. It's not the end of the world. Your audience knows you're human. Nobody expects you to be perfect.

If you make a mistake, gather yourself, make a joke, or laugh out loud to regain your composure. Then, relax and remember that you've got a great opportunity to enjoy discussing your book with a large audience.

As an author, what could be better? Have fun!

CLOSING

I wrote this resource to help you take on the media world with confidence. Now you know how to prepare for an interview, control the discussion, sell your book, and turn listeners into customers.

In addition, use the golden opportunity that interviews offer to build your author email list.

Conduct yourself like an expert, regardless if you write fiction or nonfiction.

Above all, act like an equal to the host. Use the experience to entertain, educate, and challenge the listener.

Appearing on podcasts, radio shows, or TV programs is an effective way to market your book. Employ the power of interviews to gain greater exposure, connect with new audiences, and turn listeners into happy readers.

Thank you for letting me be a part of your author journey. I wish you all the best with your books!

To your success,

Rob Eagar

Wildfire Marketing

HOW MAKE AN AUTHOR HAPPY

If you found the material in this book helpful, I'd be grateful if you took a few minutes to write a review on Amazon.

When you leave a comment on Amazon, the world's largest bookseller, it makes a huge difference to help new readers find my books. It only takes a few minutes to share your thoughts.

Your review would make my day.

Thank you!

MY FREE GIFT FOR YOU

Get three e-books to help jumpstart your book sales for FREE:

Find Readers and Sell Books on a Shoestring Budget

Mastering Book Hooks for Authors

The Ultimate Book Marketing Plan Template for Authors

Join my email newsletter and get these three e-books. Each resource can be downloaded as a file to your computer or added to any e-reader device. You will also receive my weekly e-newsletter packed with free expert marketing advice for authors.

Download these three e-books for free today at:

https://www.startawildfire.com/free-ebooks-ag

GET EXPERT HELP FOR YOUR BOOKS

Are you're tired of trying to figure out media interviews and book marketing by yourself? What if an experienced coach answered all of your questions? Get personal help from Rob Eagar, one of the most accomplished experts in America.

Author Interview Coaching

Does preparing for an interview or talking about your book may you feel confused or overwhelmed? Rob will personally teach you how to master the interview process and use the media to your advantage. The Author Interview Coaching service will teach you how to:

- Prepare for every type of interview, including podcasts, radio shows, TV appearances, etc.
- Develop enticing sound bites and talking points
- Take control of interviews, even if the host is a jerk
- Drive more book sales during an interview
- Build your email list while doing media appearances

Rob has coached numerous authors who've appeared on national television, including *Good Morning America, The Today Show, The 700 Club*, dozens of radio shows, and many popular podcasts. For details about Author Interview Coaching, visit:

https://www.startawildfire.com/author-interview-coaching

Book Marketing Master Class

What if you knew all of Rob's marketing secrets? The Book Marketing Master Class covers everything an author needs to know. Whether you're a first-time author or a seasoned bestseller, Rob will show you how to:

- Rapidly build your email list and reader audience
- Create persuasive language, including hooks, titles, and back cover copy
- Construct a complete marketing plan to maximize the book launch sequence
- Turn your author website into a 24/7 sales machine
- Maximize advertising on Amazon and Facebook
- Connect with online influencers and turn media interviews into book sales
- Discover multiple ways to create new income from your book content

Rob expertise works for fiction and non-fiction authors, first-timers and bestsellers, indie writers and traditionally-published. He will personally teach you his proven marketing techniques and apply his instruction to your specific books, goals, and experience level. Include your team and get everyone coached up at the same time. Receive follow-up access to ask questions, hold you accountable, and ensure your progress. For details on the Book Marketing Master Class, visit:

https://www.startawildfire.com/consulting/book-marketing-master-class

Personal 90-Minute Author
Coaching Sessions

Are your book sales stagnant? Got a nagging question about book marketing or publishing? Ready to raise the bar on your author career? Reach your goals by talking directly with a world-class expert. Schedule a personal 90-minute author coaching session with Rob Eagar.

Individual coaching sessions include direct access to Rob to ask questions and learn how to improve your book marketing skills. Using live video screenshare technology, he will walk you step-by-step through everything you need to know. Get immediate answers to reach more readers, build a larger audience, sell more books, and increase your author revenue. For details about purchasing a 90-minute Author Coaching Session, visit:

https://www.startawildfire.com/consulting/author-consultation

ABOUT THE AUTHOR

Rob Eagar is one of the most accomplished book marketing experts in America. He's personally coached over 1,000 authors, consulted with top publishing houses, and helped both fiction and nonfiction books hit *The New York Times* bestseller list. He even helped a book become a *New York Times* bestseller after 23 years in print!

Rob's consulting firm, Wildfire Marketing, has attracted numerous bestselling authors, including Dr. Gary Chapman, Lysa TerKeurst, Wanda Brunstetter, DeVon Franklin, Nir Eyal, and Dr. John Townsend.

In addition, he's consulted with imprints of the world's best-known publishers, such as HarperCollins, Hachette, and Simon & Schuster. Rob's industry-leading instruction can be found in *The Author's Guide* series, a collection of books dedicated to teaching authors essential marketing skills, including:

The Author's Guide to Marketing Books on Amazon

The Author's Guide to Email Marketing

The Author's Guide to Write Text That Sells Books

For more information, visit:

http://www.RobEagar.com

or

http://getbook.at/AuthorsGuideSeries

Made in the USA
Coppell, TX
24 January 2022

72256975R00052